The Dark Inside
My Hooded Coat

poems by

Mary Leonard

Finishing Line Press
Georgetown, Kentucky

The Dark Inside My Hooded Coat

ACKNOWLEDGMENTS

This Way That ~ *The Chronogram*: 2014;
Tying Knots and After Seeing Fransje Killars ~ *Ilya's Honey*: 2015;
The Blues ~ *Perfume River* 2016;
I Googled Montagano ~ *Courtship of Winds*: 2016;
Inside The Emergency Room, It's a Tough Time for Her and Roger Gene ~
A Girl: Pudding House, 2006;
After Hearing Arvo Parts's Summa for Strings, An Ode to the Clark Mill
Workers ~ *The Sweet and Low Down*: Antrim House, 2010;
Do Not Be Daunted ~ *Hubbub*: 2012, and *The World That Is*: Red Ochre
Press, 2013;
For Mark Di Savuro's Large Orange Mother Peace Sculpture ~ *Perfume
River's Anthology of Vietnam Poetry*, 2017

Publisher: Leah Maines
Editor: Christen Kincaid
Cover Art and Design: Bronwyn Gropp
Author Photo: Gerald Leonard

Printed in the USA on acid-free paper.
Order online: www.finishinglinepress.com
                also available on amazon.com

Author inquiries and mail orders:
Finishing Line Press
P. O. Box 1626
Georgetown, Kentucky 40324
U. S. A.

Table of Contents

I Googled Montagano

Nonna I never met you,
        never saw Montagano
                your Molise village
Never knew you
        but saw Montagano today on the Internet
                and want to ask, did you pick wildflowers
for your table under the olive trees?

Did you try to make the best
        of stale bread, cold coffee, the absence of greens,
                no slices of sweet red tomatoes?

Every day at lunch, you listened to the landlord's voice,
        louder than the noon time bell
                from *Santa Maria Assunta in Cielo*
What did you have for lunch? You answered Nothing

            He lists his feast
            He comes close   you smell garlic rabbit you swoon
                He steps closer   too close   so close
                    to hand sweet Nick
                        biscotti from Campobasso

Today I found this
        I can rent a cozy stone house for 38 dollars a night on Airbnb
            Nonna could it be your old house
                the one dark room cold in winter
                    no air in summer?

And this
        For sale a three story house
            with a stairway to the stars,
                a stairway of great value
I can buy your landlord's house for 300 thousand Euros!

Nonna, you were a bird of passage, an immigrant wanting to return—
              a mansion is waiting for you.

You can be the landlord now
                          hear the pigs squeal everyday

                          grow tomatoes between the stones
                plant olive trees grapevines lavender
 The Northerners won't yell terrone at you
No longer their dirtyshittypeasant

I know this
              we could go back Nonna,
                    take a ferry to the island of Termoli

Trip Advisor says
              one can take a ferry and then a water taxi to one's hotel
                    and swim in a blue pool or hike down to the one sandy
    beach
                          or one can rent a boat and row to the caves of
    white porous rock

From 2015 I see you Nonna
              swimming in your black wool dress in the blue Adriatic
                    warm so warm on this island of Termoli
 100,000 visitors come each summer,
                                the temperature 88 in July and August

Today you and I can take a helicopter for 50 Euros
         You fill your bundle with
                    wine and fresh bread   I fill my backpack with
                          water and wildflowers We climb the rocks,
                                you hiking up your skirts,
I stretching back for your hand

We disappear into the dark caverns   disappear into the unknown
                    like you did with Papa and Nick on your voyage to
        America
                            How did you know to go?
Did the town crier run down the street yelling
                                        the streets are paved with gold
        Follow me me cheap cheap chirp chirping like the tiny birds
                    the ones overhead the very ones you grabbed to wring
        their necks,
                            pull off their feathers and roast in the fire
                                eating even the small bones
Your secret like the amulets you sewed inside the folds of your black
        wool dress.

    I know this
                You Papa and Nick followed the town crier
                        on foot in carts on trains in steerage

                                        forever to Ellis island
        You traveled light   Nothing much in your bundle
                    garlic to string around your neck
                            a small vial of holy water from Santa Maria Assunta in
        Cielo

Did the dark folds of your blanket cover the smell of
        cabbagevomitshitsweat
                    Did you dream of the green and blue of Montagano
                            or the streets paved with gold?

    In Hell's Kitchen   you didn't know Dutch
                        Hell the violent swirls of water in the Hudson
                        Hell the tight dark railroad apt. where you sewed
                                for a few dollars a week
                        Hell eating stale bread drinking cold coffee.

Lonely   No landlord asked you what you ate for lunch
Violent   The Irish spit in your face Nick stole roasted potatoes
              to throw in their faces   Westside Story before guns and
    knives.

Did you dream of Montagano's pure blue air the island of Termoli
                   you never visited   as far away as America?

My treat is this
              the house dating back to the fourteenth century
                       the one belonging to nobility the one with the stone
    stairway?
I will call +39-0874-433-2230   buy the house so we can go to Termoli
            picnic on the sand eat three local meats pull apart fresh bread
            so we can both arrive.

The Blues

Mom said she cried and cried the day her baby brother died
      The day he died she felt cold as stone
The day he died the stove in their railroad flat didn't light

In Hell's Kitchen gangs called her Guinea Girl
      Mom didn't yell Mick, couldn't say that
Mom said she'd go to hell if she didn't pray
      She said Nonna wore garlic to keep the devil away

Mom said Nonna made her stir and stir the thin soup
      She said the gangs on 48th screamed go to hell!
Mom threw hot potatoes at their heads
      She heard them yell Dago Girl you smell

Mom said she wore the same smock every day
      She washed under her arms at the kitchen sink
She rubbed her skin raw with old lemon skins

Mom kissed Nonni to death when he gave her fresh rolls
      She felt warm beside Nonni delivering ice
She danced and clapped the day he gave her a china doll

She said the doll cracked to pieces when she dropped it on the tiles
      She moved the china scraps around to play pretend
Mom forgot the cold, she didn't cry, she saw daisies on a hillside

An Ode to the Clark Mill Workers

Some workers wore coveralls with pink bows
like cousins Genny and Ida in the cotton mills
spinning threads for what women could sew:
dresses and booties and fancy pieced quilts.

Genny and Ida worked in the old Clark Mills
prayed at St Rocco's and played bingo,
sewed dresses and booties and fancy pieced quilts
while suffocating and sweating in dusty dye lots

Prayed at St Rocco's and played bingo
turning cotton into lilac and clean daisy threads
working long hours in the hot Clark Mills—
suffocating and sweating in dusty dye lots

Turning cotton into lilac and clean daisy threads
Genny and Ida ate and ate their dreams away
while suffocating and sweating in dusty dye lots
and taking care of Papa and garden beds

Genny and Ida ate and ate their dreams away,
never feeling the sweat and sweetness of men
they took care of Papa and garden beds
and hid inside sun hats and flowered housecoats.

Not feeling the sweat and sweetness of men,
they tore their old skirts to wrap the fig tree
and hid inside sun hats and flowered house coats
and tied themselves to apron strings and fancy threads.

They tore their old skirts to wrap the fig tree
and planted tomatoes and basil in neat garden rows
while tying themselves into knots of string and threads
and dying alone in rooms stuffed only with pink bows.

St. Blaise: The Patron Saint of Throats

Early February. It's cold.
    The streets are freezing like sheets of thin
        metal on asphalt.

I wear cleats but slip down
    Chittenden Street. Bernadette yells
    "School is closed."

I sit on the curb remembering stories,
    The Little Match Girl dreaming about roasted geese.
    I am ready to die

in some dark land inside my hooded coat
    when a neighbor shakes me out
        like a frozen Christmas tree, and guides me home.

That night,
we slide in our grey Chevy all the way to church –
    my Dad spinning the car from curb to curb—his way
        of saying, "This doesn't exist, this feast of St. Blaise!"

But my Mom, holding suspicion and belief inside like dueling dogmas,
says, "You could get strep from sitting in the street,
    and praying to St. Blaise
is better than Vicks Vaporub."

I am scared the priest will burn my hair
    with the two candles he has to cross around my throat
        but it's easy and quick like a doctor's silver wands.

At home
Mom wraps me in flannel and says,
    "St. Blaise was a good man who escaped
        from the bad by living in a cave with wild animals

He loved them more than anyone, combing their fur
                until it gleamed like moonlight. And once he saved
                        a child from choking using only
        his hands moving them like bird's wings."

Mother told me I was lucky
                to have faith and to be wrapped in soft quilts
                        like a sparrow in her nest.
That night,
I breathed in fumes of fire and dreamed
                of candles floating around my head. I rocked
                        in fever, rocking my body to sleep,

but feeling the cool touch of white paraffin, St. Blaise's hands
                like white doves, like all the saints' hands,
                        on my holy cards.

I rocked while he combed my hair with the bones of wild beasts.
                That morning
                        I ate and ate, swallowing bacon and eggs

and all my fears of fire, sore throats,
                and the darkness inside
                        my hooded coat.

After Seeing Robert Wilson's *14 Stations* at Mass Moca
It's a Tough Time for Her

14 Stations. She could sing them, sigh them, anticipate them:
Tuck a hoe, Tuck a hoe. White Plains to Montrose, the time
to contemplate, meditate on her personal crucifixion at 14,
the curly haired wop child forced on Bronxville/Scarsdale
station stops, no Jews allowed, No Italians, Poles, Puerto Ricans.
She yearned for the elasticity of the other, the Wasp,
to be that blonde chick, content with tuna noodles and potato chips.
Her way of the cross, her hyperbolic teenage angst, tied up
in a double helix of early sixties and Catholic shit,
the priest saying, holding out his watch for all to hear
the tick, saying," Every minute someone
dies and if you are not in the state of grace, you will go
to hell, the burning fires of hell." She examined
her conscience and came up with this mortal list:
French kissing 4X, said, "fucking, bitch," took the name of God
in vain, and disobeyed, Sister Gaudentia, Mom, Dad, everyone
over 14. She examined her maroon oxfords, scuffed and untied,
and curled her kinky hair into knots, like the fist inside her gut,
and prayed, "Oh Jesus, wipe away this hell that cannot exist
without heaven." And heard Jesus answer, "Oh yes, my child"
and the priest saying, "Jesus falls a second time." She fingered
the smooth pearl beads of her rosary, meditated
on the condemnation, consolation, crucifixion. At Bronxville,
the 7th station, she exited to sort through cashmere and camel hair,
wanting to be a frozen girl, an expressionless figure like a stone,
like a boulder, to be suspended above the tracks.

Portrait in Blue

Dad worked in a printing plant
engraving toxic chemicals
into copper plates, embedding
dots with red, yellow, blue,
turning metal into shiny ads
Vogue, Harper's, Vanity Fair
selling *The Look*.

Dad could have been Chuck Close
Mondrian, Seurat, any pointillist,
but worked 9 to 5, stumbling home
from the Croton station, stinking
of benzene, but proud to slap down
proofs of slick paper so we'd know,
before any other New Yorkers, the winner
of The Miss Rheingold's Pageant.

On Sunday afternoons in our living room
he painted with oils, copying his own
Kodak photographs. I'd sit up close,
hold my breath, watch him squeeze
tubes of blues, ochres, mixing them
with turp and linseed oil, stippling
sunsets and carousel rides.

Mom said, "Wear blue, Dad will love that."
I danced in the circle of his smile,
but when I ached to hear stories
of his life as a boy in Hell's Kitchen,
Dad was crazyinsanemad from breathing in toxic
fumes* from dreaming of pixels and screens.

He couldn't remember Mom's name,
or his: Fred, Fid, Federico, only rocked
in doorways, not knowing which way to go.
In his few moments of sanity, Dad spouted
out advice as if tooling colors into copper

Make sure you have dimes in your shoe
Make sure the sky is cobalt blue
Make sure that, don't, don't let, suresuresure

*5.1 from Health and Safety Employment Act 1992 Code of Safety in Photoengraving and Lithographic processes. A probable by product of the etching action is the so called nitrous fumes, which is in fact nitrous dioxide gas.

50th Anniversary Party
"Nothing Gold Can Stay."
      Robert Frost

I wear a black shawl
      over my still fat baby belly
to mom and dad's 50th

I own the video
      me in the background
nursing my baby boy

 Dad staring into the past
      his green eyes deep
into gauging the arc of a perfect pitch

Did he know
      his sweetheart   his wife
sitting beside him?

Mom's back turns from dad
      leaning in to gossip
with her maid of honor

We all pose around the picnic table
      Uncle Dante demands, "Say cheese."
Dad smiles adjusts his shirt and tie

Sissy carries out a froufrou cake
      we all sing
Happy Anniversary   to you   to you

The baby cries   Mom cries
      and Dad says
"My birthday? Oh!" blows out

50 candles   with one long breath.

*Fire and Ice

I squat like a duck on Mom's maple dresser,
smear on lipsticks, *Fire and Ice, Peach*
on my cheeks, dots of *Ruby* around my eyes,
blend all with my hands. Mom arrives,
laughs, "You're such a girly girl!"

Older, I unfold like a heron, pull my head up
to the mirror, apply pink gloss for Global.
At night boyfriends suck sticky *Hot Coral*
like nectar from my lips. "I'm your honey
doll," I smear their pressed oxford shirts
with *Marilyn Red.*

At Iowa, I leave my lips dry, tie a scarlet
scarf around my hair. At 1:40 I slide
into a desk in Paul's *Crit.and Culture,*
sit next to the Grim Reaper, who swears he'll wear
his hooded cloak, carry his scythe until we leave
Vietnam. SDS boys with bushy beards shout,
"Be there, we're storming the Union at ten.
Dow and Marines get out!"

I wear a wool cap some guy left behind,
 bunny fur gloves, tight Doc Martins
to chant, *HeyHey LBJ, how many kids did you kill today!*
I apply *Fire and Ice,* thick on my lips and wear a Hawkeye
scarf to swing around my neck. The scarf falls backwards
when I run through the dark halls. I'm revved up
for a hot date. The bearded boys, scream, "The cops
are spraying mace." No one grabs my hand to pull me
along. I choke, cough, retreat, leave the gold scarf
to be trampled, stomped. I race for the door, exit,
toss off my cap and breathe in the freezing air.

* *Fire and Ice lipstick, first marketed by Revlon in 1952*

After Seeing Mark di Suvero's Large, Orange *Mother Peace* Sculpture

It's huge and on a ten foot high hill,
a personal statement against the Vietnam War,
"all we are saying, all we are
saaaaaing,
is give peace a chance"
...
more than statements – dreamy eyes, whispered words, "I'll be
flying over China," he said in '65.

She never heard from him again, never received a postcard that said, flying
over China, wish you were here. She forgot him but not about peace, made
some personal statements of her own, this is fuckingoveracountryapeople,
she screamed until the war was over, marched to state houses, to student
unions, to hell and back. She married, but had recurrent dreams: she
was wearing an aqua mohair sweater, a short skirt, twisting her hips back
and forth and up and down, twisting like she did last summer, drinking
bourbon like she never did before. She can't remember many things he
said, but does remember that small Tudor window, the moon so far away.
She remembers him standing there, and couldn't look away, couldn't.

And in D.C. she found him and his place of birth
and death and touched his name on that black granite wall
and heard echoes, his voice making a statement
            "See I am telling you something, something
            my name, see... my goodbye
            from that place called Nam."

Roger Gene

I find you everywhere:
on the Vietnam Wall, panel 30 E, line 008,
on the Internet Wall: *the wingman radioed, bail out.*
But do you remember twisting up and down and all around in '65?

By panel 30 E, line 008, I leave a bottle of Maker's Mark,
remembering drinking bourbon and spinning like one body in the sky.
While twisting up and down and all around in '65,
you said to me, "I'll be flying over China in July."

Remembering drinking bourbon and spinning
like one body in the sky,
You told me you loved me from head to toe,
told me, "I'll be flying over China in July."
In '70 I was flying high, shouting, *Hell no, We won't go.*

You told me you loved me from head to toe.
I married, had two kids, forgot about the stars, your kiss,
In '70 I was flying high, shouting, *Hell no, We won't go.*
You flew over Vietnam on air patrols.

I married, had 2 kids, forgot about stars, your kiss
but in the 90's saw your ghost, your spinning death grip.
You flew over Vietnam on air patrols:
Your Phantom shot down, you didn't bail out.

In the 90's, I saw your ghost, your spinning death grip,
and reached out to cry, "you never had a chance. "
The search and rescue missions circled your site twice
but I found you in the margins of all my college notes.

I reached out to cry, "you never had a chance, "
to believe, I *need to put to rest your ghost.*
I found you in the margins of all my college notes.
Your father found a piece of the Phantom at the crash site.

Your father buried your remains in Arlington,
but I still see you standing there, can't glance away,
from *Roger Gene* in the margins of my notes and
your Phantom spinning like all the bodies in the sky.

After Seeing *Figures, Colors First,* Fransje Killaars, Mass Moca

My memory—the fabric shop the cutting table,
            the dusty choke of fabric bolts
Mom's voice, don't forget, nose to end of arm for a yard!

Not the neon pink stripes of this installation
            not the green and black hearts,
                        in long lines of aqua poplin

Not the textured lime lace
            not the mannequins
                        veiled in saffron silks

This—our sewing room
            gingham and rickrack skirts
                        packs of Vogue and Simplicity

This—pinning the thin skin of patterns
            the whirr of the Singer sewing machine
                        and standing doll-still for fittings

This—be careful of how the fabric runs,
                        Be careful of plaids they have to line up!

I exit the exhibit, wrapping my head
            in an aqua and emerald scarf,
                        throwing the ends over my shoulders.
      letting it go crazy in unmatched plaids

Tying Knots

Mom crocheted,
        embroidered, knitted,
and tried to teach me how

But my fingers
        couldn't dance
across linen and wool

My mind didn't understand
        tiny stitches,
pulling flowers out of thread

In the sixties, I took up macramé,
needing
    to tie my insides in rough threads

I added beads to remember, can't get no...
        but it was the strength
of hemp that helped me

While stumbling from place to place,
carrying tangled ivy in planters
knowing they'd never find a home

Macramé was handmade, heavy,
        like the organic breads, nut butters,
bricks and boards I thought so cool

Macramé was something I could do,
something I learned in minutes
but despite the speed and ease of clumsy knots

my skill of jute and yarn and beads—
must've been a gift

something pulled from mom's
delicate hands spinning
blue forget-me-knots on linen and wool

Inside The Emergency Room

I read posters

Arrhythmia Recognition
absent, absent, absent, or present

like my life, like me
like what I'm doing tonight

absent or present, I am
neither, only a heart rate

rhythm waves, abnormal
hidden, absent, absent

I try Yoga stretches
up in Temple position

stretching to the ceiling
but I cannot be present

a wandering, a wandering
of my mind even after

reading an entire magazine
of words, words, vacant

(My mother sleeps like a baby.)

CAUTION–MEDICAL GAS SYSTEMS

I will break and enter
absent, absent, or present

Brooding on Eggs

One egg
        crack it open on the side of a blue bowl
slide into hot buttery sputtering frying pan

Do not be disturbed
        if the yolk is green or red Color depends on diet One chicken
nibbles kale, another red berries

One Easter the temperature
        reached 85 Our three year old lifted leaves of tulips
hunted beneath azaleas filled his basket with dyed eggs
        and devoured a chocolate one the yolk sugary white

One Easter I wore a blue and yellow suit   a cloche trimmed with lilies
        My sister wore green   She held a straw basket   emptied of eggs
  In two months   she would be dead

So easy to ruin an egg   one can slip on the floor
        or if one cracks the egg too fast
bits of shell mix with the whites

Eggs break in the safety of a carton before they come home
        or die before their time
Always check the expiration date

Before my expiration date
        I want to be an empty egg shell
floating under a water jet spinning in circles
        on Corpus Christi in Barcelona

Emerge whole in a golden yellow dress
        trimmed with white fur
protecting my delicate insides

Tumble to a tapas bar
        eat slice after slice of tortilla
sip glass after glass of manzanilla

Drink one, just one egg cream, letting the foam
        remain on my upper lip
And skywrite this:

There are no eggs in a NY egg cream

After hearing Arvo Pärt's "Summa" for Strings

              I hid behind
the door
              She's in there
my sister   is in there
and I'm
                     out here
hiding behind
                     the door

She does not know
                     that
         I will always hide
                              and she will always
be inside   It's dark

         I have been silent
                              So long
So long
         that I can taste my breath
and even hers.

She's inside
                     and I'm here.
I jump out.   She wants to kill me.

         I laugh, knowing   that she's
inside the door
              and I'm outside
Living for the two of us,   living as if I can
         Start   Startle
    her back   breathe
         into her,   laugh
    her back to living

Pawley's Island: The Moon, a Blood Orange

How did the Confederates fire the cannon
on Ft. Sumter when I only want to sway

in the hammock on the veranda, not lift
a finger for the lemonade on a nearby tray.

In the morning dolphins play close to shore.
At night the moon looks like a child's cutout.

At dinner the five-year-old shakes his hot dog,
I want chopped jelly fish and octopus on top!

The six-year-old asks, *If white men only like that bad man,*
does that mean Popop likes him?

The rain pounds our wooden walkway,
drowns out soft waves and kids' giggles.

The sky lightens up. On the line, our sheets
turn grey. *The Rebels are coming, The Rebels...*

The five-year-old, wrapped in a Superman towel,
jumps into the dunes, *I can save the world!*

On the news, we hear, *Lock that woman up,*
try her for treason,   make her face a firing squad!

In a hooded towel the five-year-old runs to the beach,
You can't catch me I'm the Gingerbread Man!

The sun returns, the children clamber
to the wet sand, pick up shells: oyster, scallop, clam.

A crazy sculpture of shapes—those skeletons.
At midnight the moon turns blood orange.

We drink Mint Juleps until the sun rises,
rays of light shooting up like crowns.

Do Not Be Daunted

The teacher said, Free write for 6 minutes, maybe 8

      seemed like 60—so many topics popped up
but I didn't find my way inside nor did I want to,

tired of stories
      only wanted to blither on

or become a character in a Paul Auster novel,
      watching foreign films, just watching, because who would

want to see or talk about the news:
      one woman stoned after being raped,

one whose husband threw acid in her face
      after she asked for a divorce…but those things don't just happen

      Elsewhere.

In Philly, last week, my son's friend
      was murdered by his girlfriend's stalker.

The teacher said, 6 minutes, just another minute or so.

I started to write what I didn't want to see:

The girlfriend in the car   the boyfriend dead
      on the street,

the killer driving her around
        and around

until she escaped to get the cops
        too late, always too late.

I didn't want to tell that story, any story
        I wanted to escape into writing lala sounds,
  maybe singing to Anna, the wheels on the bus go round and round.

Once on a ferry in Stockholm, reading a Paul Auster novel
        about a man watching a man watching him,

 I glanced at the woman next to me
        who was reading the same novel

and she glanced at me and we laughed
        and for a moment we were not daunted by the world's grief.

Find a place to close, the teacher said.

Dismissing the Blues

In yin yoga, we lie on our backs
    legs up the wall, arms stretched out
Someone shouts "Get the backhoe for my tush!"
    We laugh, shimmy closer, let go of doubts

Legs up the wall, arms stretched out
    The teacher says, Find your edge
I wonder   Is this too far out?
    Hold   release into the stretch

My mind says do it   Let it all hangout

The teacher says, *Find your edge*
    dabs mint on our wrists
Hold release into the stretch
      *Breathe in and trus*t

I lift my wrists smell mint watch it growing
    Chopfortea chopchop forsaladFatoush

The teacher drops mint on my third eye
    Let go of loving the good, hating the evil
Press and push do not be attached
      Breathe in and trust

Mymindswingsback NannaNonni All refugeesrunning
    thiswayandthat

The teacher says, *Let go Let go*
    of the present and the past.
My legs slide down into fields of mint.
    She says, *Press and push, do not be attached.*

My mind says Stretch stretchyourarmsout Accept
I breathe in   let go Trust thiswaythat

Mare Leonard has published chapbooks at 2River, Pudding House, Antrim House Press and RedOchreLit. Her poetry has appeared in *The Naugatuck Review, Hubbub, Cloudbank, The Chronogram, Earth's Daughter, Ilya's Honey, A Rat's Ass Review, The Courtship of Wind, New Verse News, Bindweed, Forage, Sweet Tree Review, Figroot, The Unbroken, Open A Journal of Arts and Letters* and in a collection of Vietnam poetry from Perfume River.

She recently won the First Finalist award in the NY State Di Biase Poetry Contest and Other poems will be forthcoming at *That, Ariel Chart* and *Three Elements*.

She lives in an old school house overlooking the Rondout Creek in Kingston, NY. Away from her own personal blackboard, she teaches writing workshops for all ages through the Institute for Writing and Thinking and the MAT program at Bard College.

www.ingramcontent.com/pod-product-compliance
Lightning Source LLC
LaVergne TN
LVHW021124080426
835510LV00021B/3316